I0472938

COPYRIGHT

All information in this book (Credit Management in Business) is the sole property of **Enterprise success center.**
No part of this document may be duplicated, transmitted, resold, or reproduced in any form or by any means without prior written permission from **Enterprise success center**

Enterprisesuccess09@yahoo.com
Unauthorized duplication of this document is strictly prohibited. Violators will be **PROSECUTED** to the fullest extent of the law.

INTRODUCTION

In business you will find yourself not only granting credit to your client/customers but also needing credit yourself. Granting and receiving credit could make or mar your business depending on how well you manage credit activities in your business.

The main reason a business grant credits are to increase sales, expand markets and increase the return on capital in the long term. These goals can be reached only if credit and debt collections are handled sensibly. The cost of granting credit, and of collecting debts, must justify the advantages of doing so.

The aim of this book is to provide basic guidelines for effective credit extension and debt collection in the business enterprise. If a business enterprise considers credits as a medium of exchange for goods and service: why and according to what principles must it be done to ensure that it will help the enterprise achieve its goals?

DEFINITION

Credit is part of the environment in which a business enterprise functions. The enterprise does not only give credit to its own customers, but also make use of credit itself. The enterprise uses credit to obtain funds to finance its capital requirements, for example a bank loan for the construction of a factory. Credit is also used for purchasing raw materials and stock on terms from suppliers so that the enterprise can carry on its activities (manufacturing of products it will sell). In this book we will focus on business enterprises that grants credit to its customers.

WHAT IS CREDIT

Credit is a medium of exchange to obtain goods, services or cash, at the present time, for a promise of payment in the future. The purchaser obtains goods and/or service and promise to pay the amount owed to the supplier at a later date, as agreed between them.

Instead of paying cash for the goods and services, the purchaser offers the seller a different method of payment (credit). The seller must decide whether to accept the alternative offer of payment. The seller must decide whether to accept the purchasers promise to pay in the future and supply the goods or services to the purchaser. This decision is base on the seller's assessment of the **creditworthiness** of the purchaser.

WHAT IS CREDITWORTHINESS?

Creditworthiness is a summary of all the characteristics (like willingness to pay and ability to pay) that make the purchaser's offer of future payment acceptable to the seller. It is the ability of the purchaser to obtain goods and/or services on the strength of his/her promise to pay later. The purchaser uses his/her promise (to pay later) to obtain goods, services or money.

The seller shows confidence in the purchaser by supplying goods and/or services on the strength of a promise that payment will be received in the future. The seller is not sure, however, that the purchaser will indeed make the payment in the future. There is an element of risk involved in granting credit. This risk relates to the possibility that the purchaser will not make the payment and that the seller will eventually suffer a loss (the enterprise/seller must wait for its money). It is also important to realize that an element of cost is involved in credit – it costs money to extend credit, for example the costs of financing and administrating the debtors.

If the creditworthiness of the purchaser is sufficient for the seller and the promise of future payment is accepted, a credit transaction is concluded. The credit transaction implies the following for both the seller and the purchaser:

➤ The purchaser has a duty to pay. We refer to this duty as *debt*. The purchaser is a debtor (owes the enterprise money).

➤ The seller has a right to be paid. The seller is a creditor (is owed payment by an enterprise/individual).

VARIOUS FORMS OF CREDIT

For the purpose of business organization, the following forms of credit can be distinguished:

➢ Consumer credit – credit that is granted by the enterprise when selling goods or services to the final consumer. It includes for example sales of products like clothing, stationary and medicine, as well as service like financial services (auditors and accountants), and medical services.

➢ Trade credit – credit that is granted to the enterprise by the manufacturers of product and services (like materials used in the manufacturing process), or by resellers of products and services (to the enterprise that in turn sell these products and services to other enterprises and/or final consumers).

REASONS FOR GRANTING CREIT

There are various reasons why an enterprise would consider granting credit. These reasons are linked to the advantages for the enterprise for granting credit.

ADVANTAGES OF GRANTING CREDIT

The advantages of granting credit are the following:

➢ A potential increase in sales.

➢ An increase in profits.

➢ Maintaining /strengthening a competitive position in the market.

➢ Increasing your market share.

➢ An aid to advertising.

➢ Better quality products are sold;

➤ Developing customer relations.

Let's look at each of these in details,

A potential increase in sales

The availability of credit attracts and retains customers who may otherwise not have bought from the enterprise – the enterprise attracts customers with a need for credit. Many purchasers do not have the necessary cash to buy with, but if they can use credit for purchasing, the transaction can take place. Cash buyers can also become credit customers who are prepared to spend some of their future income at the present time. The business can lose possible sales by doing business only on a cash basis – simply because many customers cannot pay cash right away.

An increase in profits

The enterprise can make more profit from an increase in sales. This is only true if the cost of granting credit is lower than the additional income gained from the credit sales. The rise in sales from the availability of credit facilities can also help the enterprise function at its best capacity, resulting in a drop in unit costs.

This has a positive effect on the profit of the enterprise.

Maintaining/strengthening a competitive position in the market

The enterprise with credit facilities is in a better competitive position to attract credit customers. If enterprises selling similar products grant credit to their customers, it can weaken the competitive position of an enterprise without credit facilities.

Increasing the market share

Continued higher sales and a stronger competitive position will result in a greater market share in the long run.

An aid to sales promotion

By granting credit the business attracts more customers, satisfies their needs and retains their custom. They always come back to buy – because they can do so on terms. On the other hand, cash customers buy from businesses offering the lowest prices – not always the same business. For example, someone with an account at a bookshop usually also buys stationary from this shop, no matter what the price are. A cash customer normally buys from whichever bookshop offers the best prices.

An aid to advertising

The business invites customers to use the credit facilities

Better quality products are sold

Credit customers are generally less sensitive to price than cash customers, and in many cases buy products of a higher quality. For example, someone buying jewelry on credit will consider buying real jewels rather than imitation jewels.

Developing customer relations

The enterprise is able to build up contacts/relationships with customers (building goodwill). The customers visit the business regularly

– like coming to pay their accounts. The business can develop loyalty among its customers.
It is thus clear that there are many reasons for a business to sell on credit.

DISADVANTAGES OF GRENTING CREDIT

We should remember, however, that credit also has certain disadvantages for the enterprise. Among these are the following:

➢ The business has to wait for its money.

➢ Certain customers may pay their bills late. This delays the settling of accounts, and means the business has to wait longer for its money in the meanwhile, the business needs money to pay its own accounts (like creditors, water, electricity, and salaries).

➢ The business has to send reminders to customers who do not pay their installments in time. Customers sometimes dislike being reminded of their debts, and this can create a negative view of credit.

> The business risk having customers not paying an account at all and being forced to write off the account as bad debt.

> Granting credit can force the business to use borrowed capital for financing debtors. This results in additional costs (like interest) for the business to meet.

> The business caries various costs connected with credit. Granting credit demands an effective system of administering and controlling accounts, which costs money. (Most of the disadvantages of granting credit can be classified as cost.)

What are the cost implications of granting credit?

The cost implications of granting credit involve the following aspects:

> The cost involve in assessing the creditworthiness of the credit applicant (the customer applying to buy on credit), the enterprise incurs costs in collecting credit information about the applicant (to decide if the

persons creditworthiness is acceptable to the enterprise). For example, an enquiry to a credit bureau or telephone calls to other trade references.

➢ The costs involved in financing the debtors. The capital used to finance credit sales could have been used in other ways (it could be invested to earn profit) if the enterprises uses borrowed capital to finance the debtors, provision must be made for paying interest on the borrowed capital.

➢ The cost of administering debtors (this leads to an increase in the running costs of the enterprise). The business must have statements printed, for example, make out accounts, post them (postage) and collect the payments – which costs money.

➢ The cost of collecting debts. Sometimes a business has extra expense recovering overdue accounts. For example, a second account must be posted, the debtors must be visited personally or a debt collecting attorney must be used.

➢ The costs involved in bad debts. If a customer does not pay his account at all and the outstanding amount does not warrant the cost of using a debt collecting attorney, it must be written off as bad debt – a loss the business has to carry.

If a business decides to sell on credit, it must be to its advantage. The costs and risks of granting credit must be carefully weighed against the advantages it offers. Granting credit raises the capital requirements of a business – the capital needed for financing the debtors, and additional administration involved in granting the credit. The business must determine whether the necessary resources exist to finance the extra capital requirements – does the business have the funds to carry the debtors? In spite of all the advantages of granting credit, financing and administering the debtors can be the main consideration in deciding whether to grant credit or not.

CREDIT AND DEBT COLLECTION POLICY

A business wanting to grant credit to its customers must consider a credit and debt collection policy very carefully. A sound credit and debt collection policy offers distinct advantages to the enterprise. The credit and collection policy gives guidance to the owner/s of a business enterprise on granting credit and debt collection are in line with the goals of the enterprise. The activities are the following:

- ➢ Assessing the creditworthiness of applicants.

- ➢ Making decisions on credit granting and setting credit limits.

- ➢ Controlling the accounts effectively.

- ➢ Effectively collecting accounts and following up overdue accounts.

EVALUATING THE CREDITWORTHINESS OF CREDIT APPLICANTS

Evaluating the creditworthiness of applicant with a view to possible credit extension is based on:

- ➢ Collecting credit information and other information about the person/enterprise; and

- ➢ Analyzing this information.

COLLECTING CREDIT INFORMATION

Where does an enterprise find the information?

The available sources of information are:

- ➢ The credit application form completed by the applicant – an order form received from an enterprise (in case of trade credit).

➢ The applicant's employer (in case of consumer credit).

➢ Trade references – other enterprises that sell to the individual/enterprise on credit.

➢ Commercial banks (the applicants' commercial bank).

➢ Credit bureaus – information on the applicants' credit record (history) can sometimes be obtained from credit bureaus.

➢ Sales representatives – an enterprise applying for credit can get information from sales representative.

➢ Annual financial statements (in case of an enterprise).

The applicant must complete a credit application form.

ANALYZING CREDIT INFORMATION

The analysis of credit information can be explained by means of the following questions:

➤ What is being/must be analyzed?

➤ Why is the analysis being done?

➤ How is the analysis done?

➤ What is the scope of the analysis?

What information is analyzed?

The following aspects are considered during the analysis of credit information (known as the C's of credit):

> **Character** – this is the willingness of the person/ enterprise to pay as agreed (are accounts paid regularly and punctually?). The customer's willingness to pay is affected by the integrity of the person/owners of the enterprise (factors like personal details, address, career/ type of business, years of service with an employer/years in business are relevant).

> **Capacity** – the applicant's ability to pay (are there sufficient financial resources available for paying regularly and on time?). In deciding whether to give an enterprise credit, the enterprise ability to pay is very important (based on information from its financial statements).

➢ **Capital** – the financial strength of the applicant (are there any reserve assets, like a savings account, which the applicant can draw on in times of financial difficulty in order to keep paying regularly and on time?).

➢ **Collateral** – security that the applicant can offer, like insurance or an asset such as a building or land.

➢ **Condition** – the current and expected economic, political and other situations and how they affect the applicant's willingness and ability to pay.

➢ **Credit history** – the applicant's history of making payments (how the applicant has handled accounts in the past).

➢ **Common sense** – the sound judgments of the person analyzing the credit data, based on his experience of credit analysis.

Why is the analysis done?

The analysis is done to establish whether the credit applicant's creditworthiness is acceptable to the enterprise or not. The enterprise must have a certain credit standard. The credit standard is an indication of the risk the enterprise is prepared to take when granting credit (the risk of non-payment of an account). The credit standard enables the enterprise to maintain a level of debtor quality such that the benefits of granting credit outweigh the risk to the enterprise. The credit standard of the enterprise is affected by factors which include:

➢ The applicant's payment record;

➢ The applicants ability to pay;

➢ The applicant's income potential;

➢ The security being offered; and

➢ The particular industry of the specific enterprise.

How is the analysis done? (Consumer credit)

In the case of consumer credit the analysis can be done using a credit granting system. Points are allocated for specific characteristics/factors like the person's income, trade references, residential address, profession, employer, and details of the applicant's bank (savings account, current account, credit card). If an applicant's points rating are equal to or higher than the minimum set by the enterprise, credit granting can be considered.

Trade credit

An enterprise's financial statements can be used in assessing its creditworthiness in terms of its ability to make payments. The integrity of its management is examined (are sound business principles followed?), the location of the business, the kind of product/services it sells, its income potential , its business risk, its history of payments, the present economic climate and the market in which the enterprise is operating.

It is also useful to compare the features and information of an individual credit application with the features and data of all the other debtors. The enterprise can see if the individual applicant has features in common with the 'good payers'. The features of the good payer can thus be used as a norm when assessing a new applicant. This stresses the importance of details concerning debtors and their credit histories.

What is the scope of the analysis?

The final goal of the analysis is to see whether the benefit of giving the applicant credit will outweigh the costs and risk involved (does the applicant meet the minimum requirements of the credit standard?). The enterprise wants complete and accurate data (as much as possible is the ideal). This data must enable the enterprise to take a decision on granting credit. The analysis is therefore done up to the point where the enterprise is ready to take a decision on granting credit. The process of collecting data must, however, be cost effective: the time and the cost used in collecting the data must be balanced against the usefulness/value of the data.

Taking credit-granting decisions and setting credit limits

Analyzing credit information leads to decisions on granting credit. Three possibilities exist, namely:

➢ Deciding to accept the credit application.

➢ Deciding to turn down the application; or

➢ Deciding to postpone a decision while obtaining more information.

The enterprise therefore has to judge whether the credit applicant's promise to pay in the future is acceptable or not. If the decision is positive, the enterprise must:

> ➢ Decide on a credit limit; and

> ➢ Inform the applicant of the credit terms or conditions of sale.

Definition:

The credit limit is the maximum amount the customer may owe the business at any given time. The customer may not buy on credit for more than this amount. Normally the credit limit can be raised. The credit limit must meet the customer's needs without leading to overspending (the customer must be able to afford the credit limit).

In case of an enterprise applying for credit (trade credit), the credit limit can initially be fixed by the value of the first order. As the enterprise shows itself to be a good credit risk, the credit limit can be reviewed (raised).

Credit terms

The credit terms of an enterprise give an indication of:

➢ The credit period – the period for which credit is granted.

➢ The cash discount (if applicable) – the discount given if the account is settled before a given time.

➢ Interest charged (if any) – the interest to be paid on an overdue account (if payment is made after the credit period has expired, interest is charged at a stipulated rate).

➢ The method of payment – in most cases, payment is made in cash or by check. Post-dated checks and stop orders are also often accepted as methods of payment. In trade credit transactions, the seller can demand bills of exchange or bank transfers (each debtor arranges that payment is made straight into the seller's bank account).

➤ The type of credit or credit plan – this is the kind of credit that is given. We distinguish between an open credit account (all purchases on the account must be paid for in full within the allotted credit period), installment/hire purchase credit (each credit purchase can be paid for by means of a deposit and for example six equal installments – finance charges are levied by the enterprise), and revolving credit (the debtor has a credit limit and must pay a specific amount on the account each month – if the balance of the account is lower than the credit limit, the debtor can buy on the account again). Credit cards are another kind of credit accepted by many businesses.

Credit contract

In the case of a formal agreement between the applicant and the enterprise the credit contract has to be in writing (for example hire purchase credit – a monthly installment including interest is payable, and if the customer does not pay, the enterprise can repossess the goods). Each of the parties must also be in possession of the contract document.

EFFICIENT CONTROL OF ACCOUNTS

To get the maximum benefit from granting credit, the business enterprise must develop an effective system of debtors' control. The business must keep a record of each transaction, nothing among others the following:

➢ The nature and volume of purchases made on credit(how active the account is)

➢ The credit limit of the account.

➢ The amount owing on the account.

➢ The debtor's pattern of payments (whether he pays regularly, slowly, or erratically).

EFFECTIVE FOLLOW-UP OF OVERDUE ACCOUNTS

The success of credit sales depends on the effective collection of debts, since the full benefits of granting credit are obtained only when the account is completely settled. The efficiency of the enterprise's debt collection policy affects the cash flow directly (which, in turn, affects the working capital position and profitability). Slow debt collection causes low cash levels, while efficient and speedy collection can raise the cash levels of the enterprise. Effective debt collection leads to a better liquidity position and in turn enables the business to make all payments to creditors regularly and on time, so improving its own creditworthiness. The efficiency of debt collection is often the difference between success and failure for the enterprise. If its cash flow is impeded by inefficient debt collection, liquidity and profitability problems can threaten its survival.

Furthermore, once the account has been settled, the business can sell to the debtor again, resulting in a positive effect on its sales.

The risks of bad debts are reduced if the collection of accounts starts as soon as possible. The longer an account is overdue, the harder it becomes to collect the accountant at the same time the possibility becomes greater that the account will never be settled at all.

Improved debt collection procedures and methods thus allow the business to keep existing accounts active, with positive effects on its cash flow and sales. The risk of unrecoverable debt is also reduced.

A business can use the following guidelines to speed up and finalize the effective collection of debts:

> Do objective credit assessments and set lower credit limits at first – lower credit limits can lead to smaller overdue accounts. Avoid credit limits that are so high that it is impossible for a debtor to pay – the credit limit must be affordable (the debtor must have the ability to pay).

> Give clear instructions on the method of payment when opening the account. The account holder must be told exactly when payment must be made, where to pay, and for example what his obligations are in terms of punctual payment. It is also worth pointing out to a debtor that inadequate or missed payments can lead to a poor credit record. Also, the business must make sure the debtor understands the statements of account.

➤ Start collecting overdue accounts immediately –
   don't waste unnecessary time before starting to
   collect an account. Inform the debtor at once that
   his account has not been paid – don't wait
   another whole month. For example, send an e-
   mail strait after the expiry date telling the debtor
   that no payment has been received. Call the
   person; if possible find out why no payment has
   been made. Visit the debtor and collect the
   outstanding money. Act in a diplomatic but firm
   manner – too threatening an attitude can drive
   good customers away, but doing nothing can
   force the business to wait too long for its money.

➤ Implement an effective system of debtor control
   to ensure immediate identification of overdue
   accounts. Regularly draw up an age analysis of
   debtors and analyze the debtor payment periods
   – be 100% informed of the exact state of affairs
   regarding the debtors, the business can see to
   what extend the real situation (regarding the
   collection of debts) agrees with the desire
   situation.

Age analysis of debtors		
% outstanding debtors	Volume of outstanding debtors	Period overdue (days)
45%	$225,000	Less than 30 days
34%	$170,000	30 – 60 days
15%	$75,000	60 – 90 days
6%	$30,000	More than 90 days
Total: 100%	$500,000	

➢ Develop a clear debt collection procedure – carry out the collection of debts according to a system and in a consistent manner. Distinguish clear stages in the procedure.

Example

The following is an example of a possible debt collection procedure:

– Send a letter to the debtor informing him that no payment has been received.

– Contact the debtor by phone to enquire why no payment has been made on his account. Try to get a payment from the debtor – negotiate with him for payment before or on a specific day. In the mean time the debtor may take no further purchases on the account (until the overdue payment has been made).

- If no progress is made with the account, the business can phone the debtor again /visit him personally.

➤ Keep a record of each debtor's payment record.

Example

- The debtor pays the correct amount.

- The debtor pays more
  per month than is expected of him.

- The debtor pays too little.

- The debtor doesn't pay his account at all.

➤ Also keep a record of every action that has been taken by the debt collection section in the enterprise and by the debtor.

➤ Shorten the follow-up time between the various stages in the collection procedure. Don't wait a month before making contact with the debtor again, for example. Follow up at regular intervals, like once a week.

➤ First concentrate on the biggest overdue accounts. The fact that account with balances are outstanding has a drastic effect on the cash flow – positive as well as negative. Why? If a large overdue account cannot be recovered, it means that the enterprise loses a large cash sum from its cash flow, and likewise if a large overdue account is collected, the cash flow surges. Large outstanding amounts can have a serious negative effect on the cash flow of an Enterprise.

➤ Keep special conditions of sale and special arrangements like extended credit periods and reduced monthly installments to a minimum. These arrangements slow down the collection of accounts.

➤ Limit possible problems with collections like erroneous accounts or accounts that are posted too late.

➤ Ensure that data concerning customers is constantly updated (address, telephone numbers, etc). Also obtain new credit information (from other businesses, credit bureau) as soon as an account shows collection problems.

➤ Act in such a way that the relationship with the customer stays unspoiled – keep the customer's goodwill. The business must keep the account, and the customer must still want to buy from the business. Encourage proper telephone etiquette and ensure that the customer is treated decently. The way the customer is treated can be the deciding factor in the settlement or non-settlement of an account.

CONCLUSION

In this book we discussed credit management which includes various forms of credit. The advantages and disadvantages of granting credit, including the cost of credit, were discussed. We stressed the importance of the following sound principles in granting credit and in debt collection procedures. We saw that an enterprise must consider whether credit will in fact be to the benefit of the business, and if it does so, it must structure its policy for granting credit and collecting debts.

Attention must be given to:

➢ Assessing the creditworthiness of credit applicants.

➢ Taking credit decisions, setting credit limits and providing information on credit terms.

➢ Effective account control.

➢ Effective collection of accounts and following up of overdue accounts.

About Enterprise success center

The **Enterprise success center** is a business management consultancy firm Established to promote the successful establishment, running, survival and growth of businesses globally.

As the global recession last we are certain we've been the strength behind the survival of many businesses that would have otherwise gone under.

We develop practically applicable real-time business solutions that meet specific needs of each enterprise we work with.

We've developed solutions in areas such as;

- Starting a business

- Financial management

- Product development

- Branding

- Marketing

- Strategic business development

- Competition

- Budget drafting.

➢ Credit management.

➢ ETC

At the **Enterprise success center** we succeed only if you've succeeded.

Contact us now at;

Enterprisesuccess09@yahoo.com
Please tell us your opinion of our work.

THANK YOU FOR PURCHASING THIS BOOK.

We sincerely hope it has been of great value to you.

www.ingramcontent.com/pod-product-compliance
Lightning Source LLC
Chambersburg PA
CBHW071553170526
45166CB00004B/1655